PICTUREPEDIA

NOTE TO PARENTS

This book is part of PICTUREPEDIA, a completely
new kind of information series for children.
Its unique combination of pictures and words
encourages children to use their eyes to discover and
explore the world, while introducing them to a wealth
of basic knowledge. Clear, straightforward text
explains each picture thoroughly and provides
additional information about the topic.

'Looking it up' becomes an easy task with
PICTUREPEDIA, an ideal first reference for all types of
schoolwork. Because PICTUREPEDIA is also entertaining,
children will enjoy reading its words and looking
at its pictures over and over again. You can encourage
and stimulate further inquiry by helping your child
pose simple questions for the whole family to
'look up' and answer together.

TRANSPORT

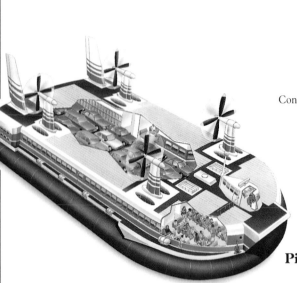

A DORLING KINDERSLEY BOOK

Conceived, edited and designed by DK Direct Limited

Consultant Eryl Davies

Project Editors Francesca Baines
Seán O'Connell
Art Editor Sarah Goodwin

Series Editor Sarah Phillips
Series Art Editor Ruth Shane

Picture Researcher Miriam Sharland

Production Manager Ian Paton

Editorial Director Jonathan Reed
Design Director Ed Day

First published in Great Britain in 1994
by Dorling Kindersley Limited
9 Henrietta Street
London WC2E 8PS

Reprinted 1997

A CIP catalogue record for this
book is available from the British Library.

ISBN 0-7513-5119-9

Reproduced by Colourscan, Singapore
Printed and bound in Italy by Graphicom

TRANSPORT

DK

DORLING KINDERSLEY

LONDON • NEW YORK
STUTTGART

CONTENTS

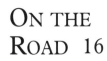

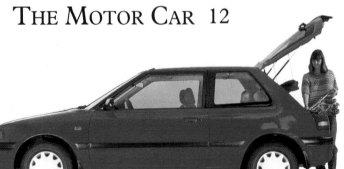

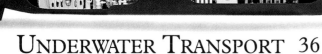
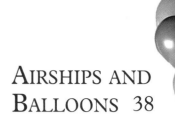

WHAT IS TRANSPORT?

Transport is so much a part of your life that you probably take it completely for granted. People have relied on transport from the very earliest times and without it the modern world would grind to a halt. Millions of people would not get to work, many children would not get to school and things would not be delivered to shops. Even the letters you send would never reach their destinations.

Round Trip
Transport has helped people to understand the world. In the 16th century, the Portuguese sailor Ferdinand Magellan led the first trip around the world. He brought back exotic spices and the first facts on how big the Earth was.

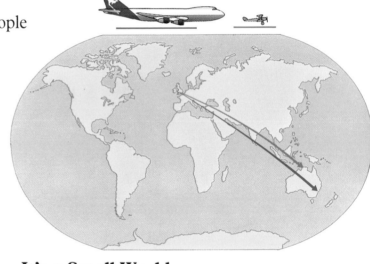

Cloves

Nutmeg

It's a Small World
Thanks to modern transport, the world seems smaller all the time. When Amy Johnson flew her Gypsy Moth aeroplane from England to Australia in 1930, it took 20 days. In 1989 a Qantas Boeing 747 flew from England to Australia in just over 20 hours!

Special Delivery
The postal service uses many different forms of transport. You can see some of them by following a letter from Canada to the Scilly Isles.

It leaves Toronto's airport by jumbo jet.

A truck takes it from the airport to a sorting office.

It travels by underground 'mail rail' across London.

Next, it goes to Plymouth on a Royal Mail train.

Be Prepared

There is no point in setting off anywhere unless you know where you are going. Maps show you what direction, and how far, you must travel to reach where you want to go.

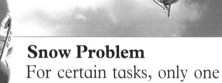

Snow Problem

For certain tasks, only one type of transport will do. A helicopter may not be able to land to make an emergency airlift, so a sledge is used to carry the injured skier to safety.

Wheel Good Time

Transport isn't just for getting from one place to another. With a little bit of practice it can be a lot of fun, too!

Time Is Money

Millions of people all over the world depend on transport to get to work every day. If the transport system breaks down, people cannot do their jobs and so money is lost.

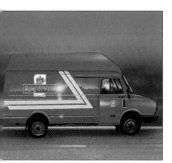

Then a van rushes it to the town of Penzance . . .

. . . for a short journey over the sea by helicopter.

On the Scilly Isles, a small van takes it to be sorted.

It finally reaches its destination on a bicycle.

ANIMAL TRANSPORT

Express Post
In America in 1860 a mail service called the Pony Express was set up. It delivered the mail faster than ever before.

Until animals were domesticated, people had to carry everything themselves, and most people did not travel very far. The first animals used for transport were probably dogs, but the most important have been horses. First they carried loads on their backs and then they pulled carts. Like cars today, the number and type of horses a person owned became a sign of their wealth.

Pollution Problems
In the 19th century, horses usually worked in shifts. So as well as all the horses on the streets, there were many others resting in stables. In busy cities like London, all these horses caused a very smelly pollution problem.

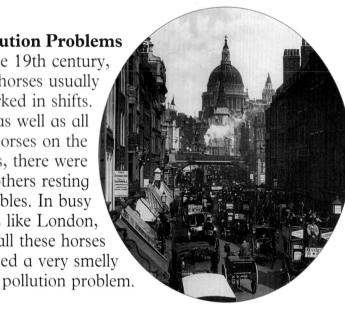

The driver steers the dogs by shouting instructions to them.

The sledge slides over the surface of the snow.

Horse Power
Teams of horses were once used for jobs such as ploughing and harvesting. Engines are still measured in a unit based on the pulling power of one working horse. This unit is known as horsepower.

On Patrol
In many countries, such as Spain, police forces still use horses. They are ideal for controlling crowds.

Whatever the weather or countryside the rider drove the horse at top speed.

The number of huskies in a team depends on the size of their load.

Keeping hold of the sealed mail pouch, the rider jumped on a fresh horse at each stage.

Just a few seconds later the rider set off to the next stage.

Animals in Action
Animals are still used in many parts of the world for carrying people or goods.

An ox in Chad

Huskies have thick winter coats to keep them warm. At night they dig themselves beds in the snow.

The only fuel huskies need is food, which can be hunted along the way.

An elephant in India

The dogs at the front, called lead dogs, are the most experienced.

A llama in Peru

Ships of the Desert
Camels are perfectly adapted for living in hot, dry conditions. For many centuries the nomads living in the deserts of the Middle East have used them for transport.

A yak in Tibet

BIKES

Bicycles were invented in the late 1700s. But they have changed their shape so much over the years that some early bikes such as the 'ordinary' bicycle, also called the penny-farthing, look very strange to us today. Power for a bicycle comes from the rider but sometimes the rider simply runs out of energy! In 1885 a German, Gottlieb Daimler, added an engine to the bicycle and so the motorbike was invented. The very first motorbikes had tiny steam engines, but today they have petrol engines and can more than match cars for speed.

Fix it Yourself
Bicycles are simple machines and one of the cheapest forms of transport. Most faults with bicycles are quite simple, too, and can be repaired cheaply and easily by their owners.

Pollution-Free Traffic
There are around one billion bicycles in China, and in the rush hour in Shanghai there is a crowd of bicycles as people ride home. Imagine the terrible fumes and the effect on the environment if all these cyclists drove cars instead of pollution-free bicycles.

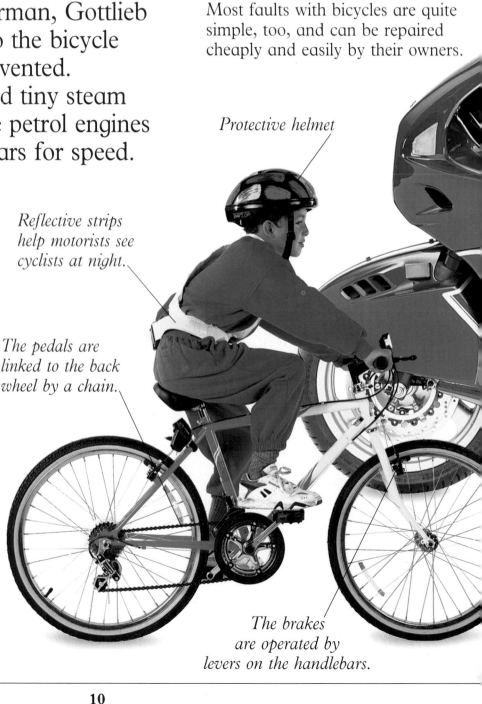

Protective helmet

Reflective strips help motorists see cyclists at night.

The pedals are linked to the back wheel by a chain.

The brakes are operated by levers on the handlebars.

Riding a motorbike can be dangerous and a rider should wear leather clothes and a special helmet for protection.

Working Bikes

Scooters, which are motorbikes with small engines, are used for many jobs around the world. The Spanish Post Office uses yellow scooters for delivering much of its post. Bicycles can also be adapted for carrying all sorts of things – even pigs!

There are storage compartments under the seat.

This part can be removed to make a seat for a passenger.

Hot Wheels

Motorbikes come in all shapes and sizes for different jobs and sports.

World War II
US Army motorbike

1966 police motorbike

1983 Racing motorbike

The panels of this motorbike are shaped so the bike will cut smoothly through the air. Its top speed is 238 kilometres an hour.

The motorbike engine runs on petrol.

The exhaust carries waste fumes from the engine.

Motocross motorbike

THE MOTOR CAR

The first cars looked very different from cars today. They were like carriages, but powered by petrol engines instead of horses, and very slow and difficult to drive. They were even harder to stop, and every car had a horn to hoot as a warning to other people. But the car was here to stay and gradually became more like the cars we drive today.

Red Alert
Early cars were thought to be so dangerous that a man with a red flag had to walk in front of them.

Folding bonnet

Engine

This car was made in 1896 by a company that also made bicycles.

Protective Clothing
Early cars were completely open and the roads were rough and dusty. So early motorists had to dress up well to protect themselves from the rain, cold and dirt.

On early cars many bicycle parts were used, such as this chain and spoked wheels.

Hand brake

Horn

A Convoy of Cars
Over the years, the shape of cars has changed a lot.

Rolls-Royce Silver Ghost

Cadillac

Bugatti

Austin Ten

A Car for the People

To begin with, only the very rich could afford to buy cars. But in 1908 an American, called Henry Ford, produced the Model T – a car for ordinary people. They were made in factories in huge numbers and were painted black. They were cheap and he sold 250,000 in the first five years.

These 'handlebars' were used to steer the car.

The seats of this car all face inwards, just like the seats in a horse-drawn carriage.

Early cars had solid tyres instead of the pneumatic tyres we use today.

Basket

Gear lever

The American Dream

After the Second World War there was a boom in the car industry in America. Marvellous machines were created, like the Cadillac Coupé de Ville, which was six metres long. Americans became so attached to their cars they took them everywhere, even to special 'drive-in' restaurants and cinemas!

Volkswagen Beetle

Citroën 2CV

Chevrolet Corvette

Mercedes-Benz 'Gullwing'

CARS TODAY

It is hard to imagine a world without cars. They are all around us and are always being improved to make them more comfortable, more reliable, faster and safer. And cars must continue to change. There are now so many cars in the world that they are one of the greatest threats to our environment. Experts are constantly thinking of new ways to make affordable cars that use less energy and produce less pollution.

Safety First
Engineers test all new car designs for safety by crashing the car and filming what happens to dummies inside. Some cars have airbags in the steering wheel that inflate in a fraction of a second in a crash.

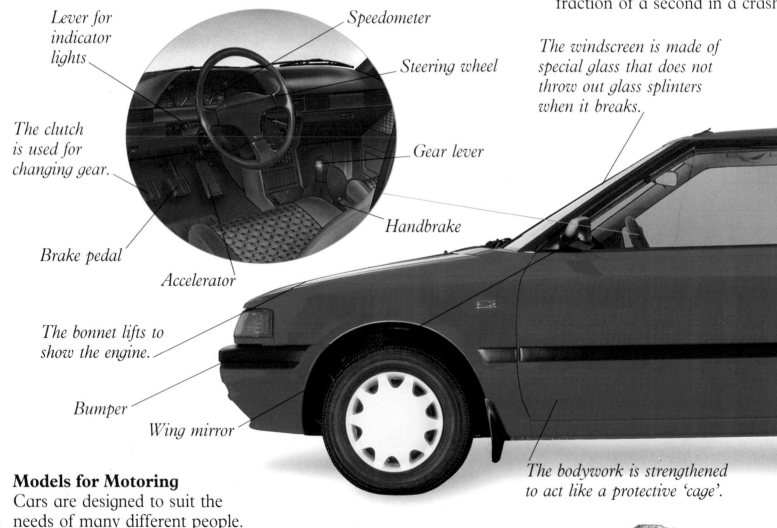

Lever for indicator lights

Speedometer

Steering wheel

The clutch is used for changing gear.

Gear lever

Brake pedal

Handbrake

Accelerator

The windscreen is made of special glass that does not throw out glass splinters when it breaks.

The bonnet lifts to show the engine.

Bumper

Wing mirror

The bodywork is strengthened to act like a protective 'cage'.

Models for Motoring
Cars are designed to suit the needs of many different people.

Mini car

Saloon car

Sports car

Family car

Record Breaker

In 1983, a jet-powered car called *Thrust 2* reached 1019.25 km/h. It had aluminium wheels but no tyres because at that speed, tyres would tear to shreds.

Sticking to the Road

Racing cars have low bodies, an aerofoil or 'wing' at the back that pushes the car down, and wide, gripping tyres. These are all designed to keep the car firmly on the road at speeds of up to 320 kilometres an hour.

This door opens wide so that luggage can be stored in the back.

Young children must sit in special seats that hold them safely in place.

Future Energy

Most petrol engines are quite noisy and give off harmful fumes. Quieter and cleaner electric cars are now being designed. But their batteries need recharging after a short distance so they can only really be used in the city.

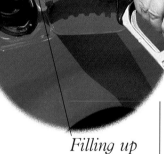

Filling up with petrol

These lights are used to tell the driver behind if the car is going to turn, brake or reverse. They also show where it is in the dark.

Knobbly tyres grip the road in all weathers.

Pick-up truck

Stretch limousine

Camper van

זהירות! מטען חורג

ON THE ROAD

As roads all over the world become more and more crowded, people are beginning to realise that a good road system is just as important as the vehicles themselves. Different types of roads are needed for different situations. Freeways, or motorways, are designed to keep long-distance traffic moving. In towns, cars must stop to let other traffic pass, and obey the instructions given by signals such as traffic lights.

Keeping Things Moving
Traffic lights usually work to a set pattern, so in tricky situations the best traffic controllers are people.

Endless Roads
America holds the record for having the greatest length of road in the world – more than six million kilometres. That is the same distance as driving around the Earth's equator 150 times.

Freeways keep traffic off narrow city streets.

This freeway is in Los Angeles, in the United States, where traffic drives on the right-hand side of the road.

Digging Deep
More than 100 different types of machines are used to build a motorway.

Human Traffic
In Britain, people known as lollypop men and women help children to cross dangerous roads outside schools.

Without Words

Road signs must be quickly understood by all drivers, whatever their language and even if they cannot read.

Watch out for elk

No right turn

Petrol station

Slippery road ahead

This is a city road in Leeds, England, where cars drive on the left.

Warning signs direct traffic round road works.

Pedestrians can cross roads safely by using a bridge.

Markings on the road show drivers which lane they should take.

To avoid sharp bends, link roads often form large curves.

Cars do not have to stop where two freeways cross because one road passes over the other.

Slip roads lead cars off the freeway.

Car-Free Zones

In some cities, like Copenhagen in Denmark, streets have been closed to traffic so that people can enjoy shopping in safety.

Clamping Down

Bad parking can cause traffic jams. In some countries, a car parked illegally will have one of its wheels clamped. This puts the driver off parking there again.

Hold-Up Headache!

All the energy-saving advantages of cars today are lost if they cannot drive at the most efficient speeds. So traffic jams do not just drive you mad, they cause pollution, too.

Buses and Trams

'Bending' Bus
A 'bending' bus carries more people than a normal bus – up to 180. An extra passenger wagon is added to the main vehicle, and 'bends' at the join when the bus turns corners.

Once, people had to walk or ride on horseback to work, but as towns grew, new forms of transport were needed to take people long distances to offices, shops or schools. Buses and trams were the answer to this problem. In the 19th century, buses and trams were pulled by horses. By the early 20th century, buses had engines and trams had electric motors, and fleets of them were needed to cope with the population of the growing cities.

Lift-up roof ventilator

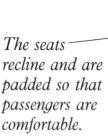

The seats recline and are padded so that passengers are comfortable.

Trams in Town
Trams run on rails in roads. The first ones were pulled by horses through New York City in the United States in 1832. Today, electric-powered trams trundle up steep streets in San Francisco in the United States and through Amsterdam in Holland.

Jeepneys
Small buses can cope with busy streets better than big buses. The colourful jeepneys of the Philippines weave their way in and out of traffic.

Upstairs and Downstairs
The big red double-decker buses of London are famous all over the world. They can carry up to 91 passengers and are still thought to be the best way of moving large numbers of people quickly and easily across the city.

Room on Top?
Buses are vital to the lives of people living in developing or remote regions of the world. They take children to school and farmers to market. Buses are often so full that passengers have to travel on top with the baggage!

Videos can be viewed

Machines for making tea and coffee

Curtains can be drawn when people want to sleep.

Coach Comfort
Unlike buses, coaches are designed for taking people on long trips. They have a more powerful engine, better seating and more space. Modern express coaches often have toilets, air conditioning and even videos.

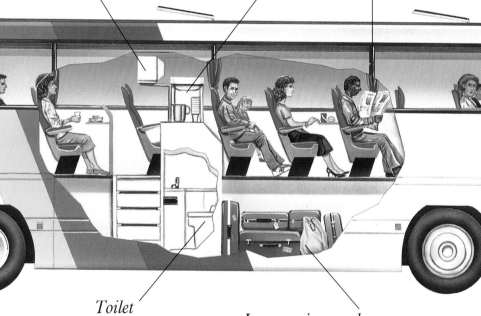

Toilet

Luggage is stored under the floor.

The windows are tinted and double glazed.

The driver sits on a lower level to be closer to the road.

All For You
Taxis come in all sorts of shapes – on land and water!

Italian gondola

Indian rickshaw

Thai tuk-tuk

British black cab

TRUCKS

Trucks come in all shapes and sizes and do very different jobs. Some trucks are very specialized and are used for essential services like collecting rubbish and fighting fires. Most trucks, however, are used for transporting goods. Trucks are ideal for this job as they can deliver right to the door. Even things carried by trains, planes and boats usually need trucks to take them on the last stage of their journey.

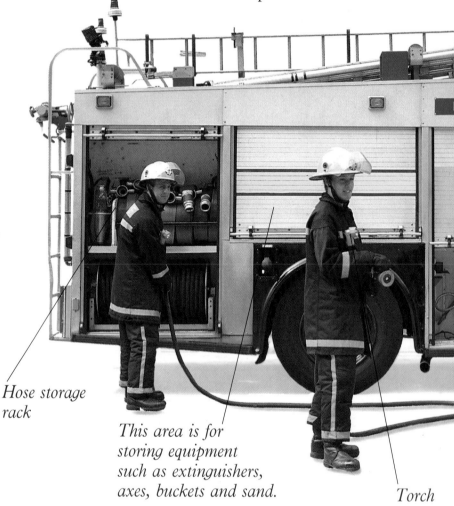

Semi-trailer

Tractor

Tight Corners
Long trucks are often made up of two parts that are hinged so they can turn tight corners. The front part is called the tractor and it pulls a semi-trailer.

Floodlight for night emergencies

Warning light

Hose storage rack

This area is for storing equipment such as extinguishers, axes, buckets and sand.

Torch

This gauge shows how much water is left in the fire engine.

Pump for the fire engine's internal water supply

Trains Without Tracks
Some of the world's biggest trucks are used to transport goods across the desert in Australia. They are called roadtrains because one truck pulls many trailers.

Big Trucks

Amphibious truck

Cement truck

Earth mover

Car transporter

The equipment for cutting people out of crashed cars is stored in here.

The ladder can be raised automatically to a height of 13.5 metres.

Blue flashing light

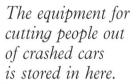

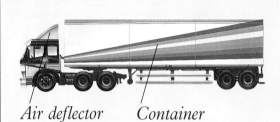
Air deflector   Container

A Working Arrangement
The same tractor can hook on semi-trailers of many different types, so no journey is wasted. Air deflectors make some loads more streamlined to save fuel.

Tanker

Five crew members can sit in the front and rear of the cab.

This reflective strip makes the fire engine easy to see.

Over the Top
Trucks are not just used for work. People often race them and perform crazy stunts with them, too. This Big Foot truck is demonstrating how to flatten a row of parked cars!

Cab Comforts
At night, long-distance truck drivers usually sleep in their cabs, in an area behind the seats. Some have only bunks, but others have televisions, fridges and even ovens.

STEAM TRAINS

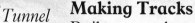

Tunnel

The first steam trains were built at the start of the 19th century. At first, people were frightened by these big, noisy and smoky machines. But locomotives soon became a familiar sight in many countries, particularly America. By 1840, half the total track in the world was in the United States.

Making Tracks

Railway tracks need to be as straight and even as possible. They go through, over or around any obstacles in their way.

Rocket on Rails

In 1829, Robert Stephenson's *Rocket* won an important locomotive contest at Rainhill, England. It signalled the end of horse-powered transport.

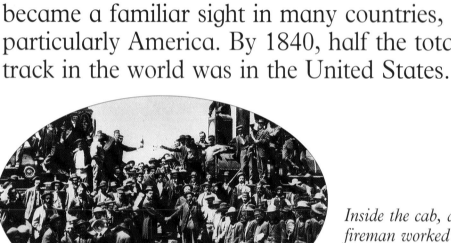

Meeting in the Middle

In 1863, rail workers began laying a track from both the east coast and the west coast of America. Six years later, the two tracks came together in the state of Utah.

Inside the cab, a fireman worked beside the driver, feeding the firebox with coal.

The steam whistle gave warning signals.

Water turned to steam inside the boiler.

This American steam train dates from 1875.

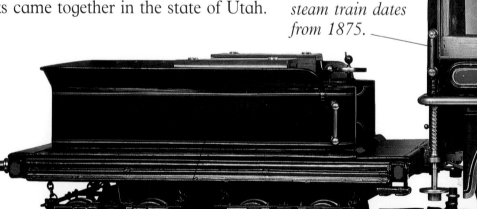

The tender held coal for the fire and water for the boiler.

The connecting rod turned the big driving wheels.

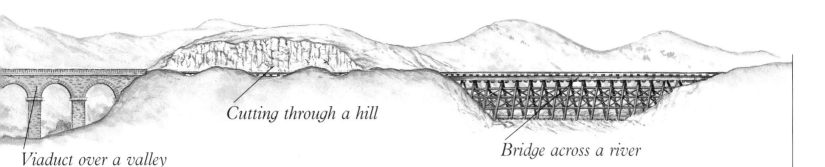

Viaduct over a valley

Cutting through a hill

Bridge across a river

Wasted Energy

Keeping a steam locomotive moving is very hard work for the fireman because so much of the heat and steam from the burning coal is wasted. From this pile of coal, only the shovelful will power the train, the rest is wasted.

7 kilograms are used.

93 kilograms are wasted.

A large headlamp helped the driver to see ahead at night.

Grand Tours

In 1865, American furniture maker, George Pullman, started fitting trains with luxury dining and sleeping carriages. Expensive 'Pullman cars' became popular in the US and in Europe.

In the cylinder, a piston converted the steam into mechanical power.

The steel guard on the front was called a cowcatcher. It pushed stray cattle or buffalo away from the track!

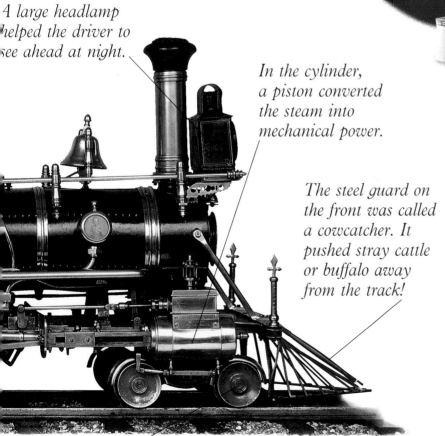

This 'bogie' stopped the train derailing on bends.

Still Steaming

Steam trains still work for a living in countries such as India and China. Locomotives also haul passengers and produce across vast distances in Africa and South America.

ELECTRIC AND DIESEL TRAINS

In 1964 the Japanese opened the first high-speed electric railway. These 'bullet' passenger trains reached speeds of 210 kilometres an hour, a world record at that time. But railway companies earn most of their money by moving goods, called freight. Freight trains are often pulled by diesel locomotives and they keep a lot of traffic off the roads. The world's longest freight train, in South Africa, had 660 wagons and was over seven kilometres long!

Round the Bend
Most trains only travel at top speeds on straight tracks. But in Italy they have designed a train that tilts inwards on curves. This means it doesn't need to slow down much on bends.

On electric trains, the section that pulls the carriages is called a power car.

The Inter-City Express, or ICE, is an electric train from Germany.

Pantographs pick up electricity from overhead wires to power the train.

Diesel Power
Like this long Canadian railway convoy, many passengers and goods still travel by cheaper, diesel-powered trains.

The French electric high-speed train is called the TGV. On its regular route it has a top speed of 300 km/h.

High-speed train routes are expensive to set up because they need a special track that has gentle curves.

At the Controls

The control centre for TGVs in Paris is in contact with the driver of every train. Controllers can warn the driver about any problems ahead, such as hold-ups, signal failures and electrification faults. In this way, the control centre keeps the rail network running as smoothly as possible.

Grand Central Station

The largest railway station in the world is Grand Central Station in New York. It has two levels with 41 tracks on the upper level and 26 tracks on the lower one.

On the Tracks

A great variety of engines and wagons use the railway tracks of the world today.

An ICE has two power cars and can carry up to 500 passengers in twelve carriages.

Breakdown train

Snow plough

Coast to Coast

One of the great railway journeys of the world crosses Australia, from Sydney to Perth. The route covers 3,968 kilometres in three days and along the way includes a world record – 478 kilometres of completely straight track!

Passenger train

The streamlined shape of electric trains helps them speed along. In tests the ICE has reached 345 km/h.

Freight train

UNDERGROUND AND OVERGROUND

As a city grows busier, the traffic on the roads becomes heavier and slower. This problem can often be solved by building a railway across the city, either over it, on tracks raised above the roads, or under it! There are underground railways all over the world, from London, which has the longest with 408 kilometres of route, to Moscow, where stations are like palaces. But they all do the same job – keep people moving.

No Smoking
The first underground railway opened in London in 1863. It used steam trains but the smoke often made it impossible to see in the tunnels. The answer was electric trains, which were introduced in 1890.

A Tight Squeeze
So many people travel on the underground railway in Tokyo, Japan, during the rush hour, that special 'shovers' are employed to squeeze passengers into the trains.

The London Underground is also called the 'tube' because the deep tunnels are built using steel tubing. Tunnels near the surface are dug like ditches and then covered over.

Emergency stairs

Underground trains are powered by electricity picked up from special rails.

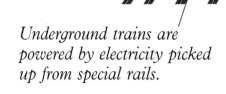

Signs tell people where there is an underground station.

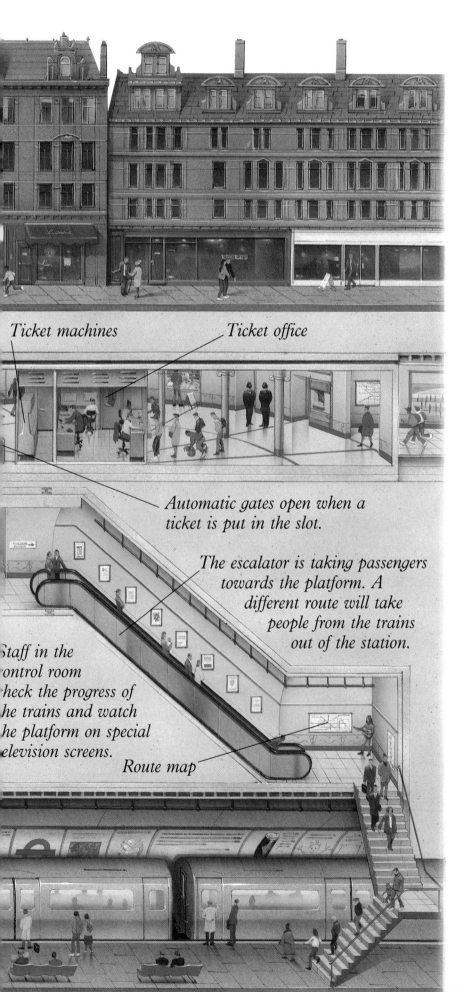

Ticket machines

Ticket office

Automatic gates open when a ticket is put in the slot.

The escalator is taking passengers towards the platform. A different route will take people from the trains out of the station.

Staff in the control room check the progress of the trains and watch the platform on special television screens.

Route map

Riding a Single Rail

It is not always possible to build an expensive underground railway system, so some railways run overground. In Sydney, Australia, some trains run on top of a single rail, called a monorail.

Hanging On

Not all trains run on top of the rail. The first monorail was built in Wuppertal, Germany, and the electric trains hang from the line.

Going Up!

Special types of transport are needed for getting people up steep slopes.

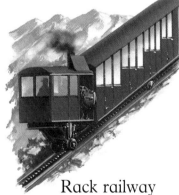

Rack railway

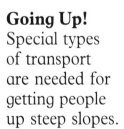

Cable car

Funicular railway

CANALS AND RIVERS

Mississippi steamboat

Large rivers have always been lifelines linking one part of a country to another. From the very earliest times they were used as trade and supply routes. But as trade and industry grew, so did the demand for more and more waterways. As a result, special waterways, called canals, had to be built. These canals linked together towns, rivers and even seas.

Europort
Rotterdam in the Netherlands is one of the world's largest and busiest ports. From here, at the mouth of the river Rhine, huge barges heaped with grain, coal and metals travel upriver into Germany's industrial centres.

Streets of Water
The Italian city of Venice has canals instead of streets. Cars and trucks can't float, so boats are the best way to travel in this watery city. People go to work or school by riding on gondolas and motorboats. Shops have their produce delivered by boats too.

A Tight Squeeze
Narrow boats were designed to pass through narrow locks on English canals. Once they carried goods, but now most are used for pleasure.

Cabins are often decorated with painted roses or castles.

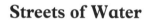

Early Boats

On many great rivers, boats have not changed in design since the earliest times.

A sampan on the Yangtze, China

A felucca on the Nile, Egypt

A dugout canoe on the Amazon, Brazil

Just Passing Through

Locks on canals allow boats to move from one water level to another.

Lock gates open

Lock gates closed

When the water is level, the upper lock gates open to let the boat in.

Lock gates closed

Valves open

Valves on the lower gates let water out of the lock.

Lock gates open

Lock gates closed

The boat moves out when level with the lower section.

The Big Short Cut

The Suez Canal was opened in 1869. It joins the Mediterranean to the Red Sea and is more than 160 kilometres long. It means that ships no longer have to sail thousands of kilometres around Africa to get from Europe to the Far East.

Floating Homes

Many people live on canals. In Amsterdam there are thousands of houseboats moored all year round.

A shallow hull means the boat can move through water that is not very deep.

This narrow boat has four beds, a kitchen and a bathroom.

The tiller moves the rudder.

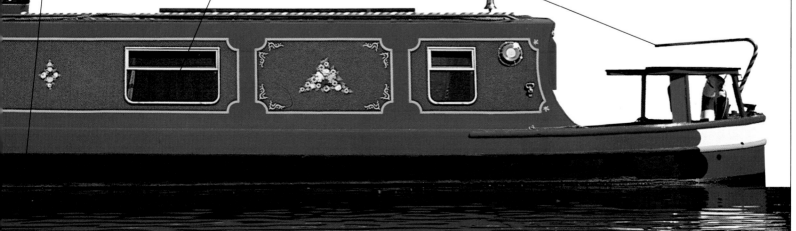

SAILING SHIPS

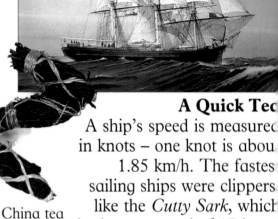

Nearly three-quarters of the Earth's surface is covered by water, most of it in the seas and oceans. For thousands of years people have been finding ways to cross this water. At first they built rafts, and boats with oars, but around 2900 BC the Egyptians began to use sails. From then on, sailing ships ruled the seas until a century ago. Today, big ships have engines, but small sailing ships are used for sport, fishing and local trade.

China tea bundles

A Quick Tec

A ship's speed is measured in knots – one knot is abou 1.85 km/h. The fastes sailing ships were clippers like the *Cutty Sark*, which had a top speed of 17 knots (31 km/h). It transported tec from China to England ir about 100 days

Using a sextant, sailors can find their way when they are in the middle of the ocean from the position of the Sun or the stars.

Sea Charts
The sea often hides dangers, like shallow waters or shipwrecks, so sailors must find their way using sea maps, called charts. These also show other information, like the route a ship must take to avoid other ships.

Tall Ships
Many of the great ships of the past have been restored and are used today for special 'Tall Ships' races.

Across the Ocean
For hundreds of years sailing ships have travelled the oceans of the world for exploration, trade and war.

15th-century Portuguese caravel

16th-century Spanish galleon

17th-century merchant ship

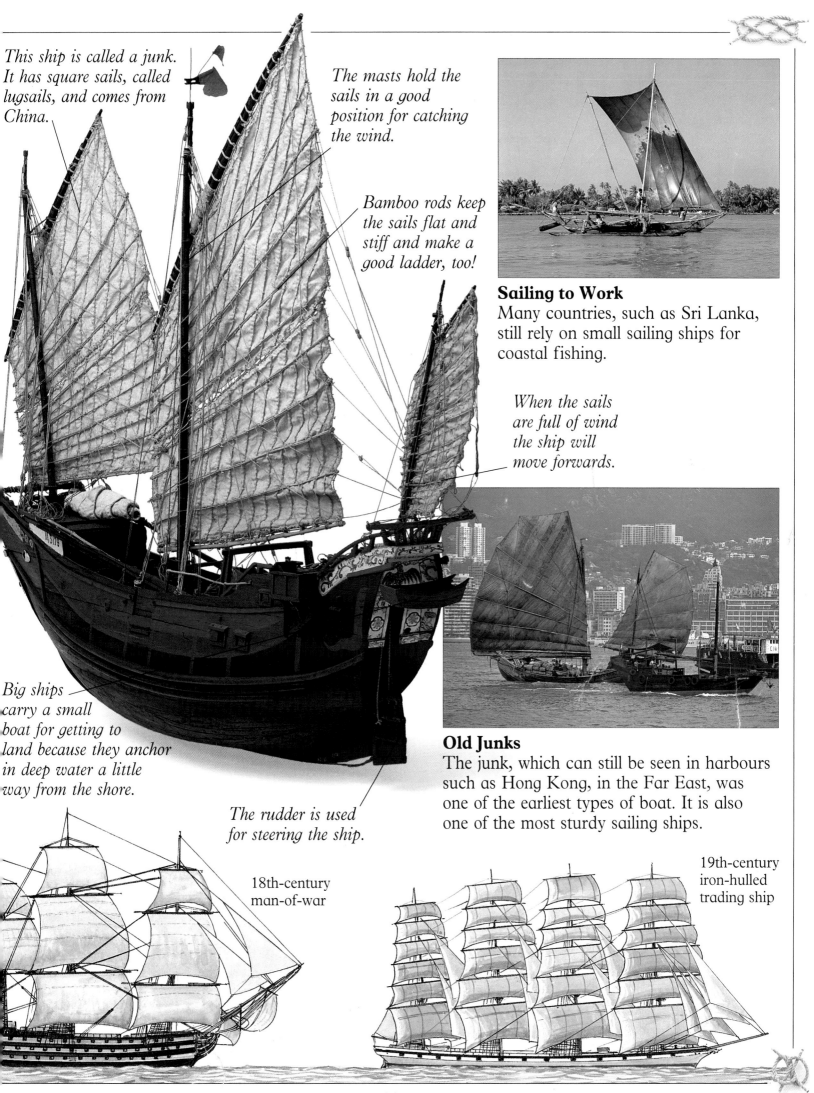

This ship is called a junk. It has square sails, called lugsails, and comes from China.

The masts hold the sails in a good position for catching the wind.

Bamboo rods keep the sails flat and stiff and make a good ladder, too!

Big ships carry a small boat for getting to land because they anchor in deep water a little way from the shore.

The rudder is used for steering the ship.

Sailing to Work

Many countries, such as Sri Lanka, still rely on small sailing ships for coastal fishing.

When the sails are full of wind the ship will move forwards.

Old Junks

The junk, which can still be seen in harbours such as Hong Kong, in the Far East, was one of the earliest types of boat. It is also one of the most sturdy sailing ships.

18th-century man-of-war

19th-century iron-hulled trading ship

SHIPS WITH ENGINES

Wind is not a very reliable form of power – sometimes it blows from the wrong direction and sometimes it does not blow at all! But from around 1800, steam engines were used to turn paddle wheels or propellers. Steam power moved ships faster and was a more reliable way of transporting people and goods. Today, ships use mainly diesel engines and their most important job is carrying cargo.

Propeller Power
The ship's engine turns a propeller at the back of the ship. This pushes the ship forwards. On a big ship these propellers can be enormous.

The ship is steered from the wheelhouse.

Living quarters

This part of the ship is called the bridge.

The cruising speed of a ship like this is around 15 knots or 28 km/h.

In the Dock
In modern ports, like Singapore, most cargo arrives on trucks and trains and is already packed in containers. These are stored on the dockside and can then be neatly loaded onto the ships using cranes.

Pull and Tug
Big ships are difficult to control and from full speed can take several kilometres just to stop. So in ports and harbours small, powerful boats, called tugs, help push and pull big ships safely into position.

A Holiday at Sea

Cruise ships offer passengers a luxury holiday as they travel. One of the best-known cruisers today is the *Queen Elizabeth II*. It can hold 1,800 passengers and 1,100 crew.

A Loading Line

On the side of a ship is a row of marks called a Plimsoll line. A certain one of these marks must always be above water or the ship may sink. There are several marks, as ships float at different levels in salt or fresh water, in summer or winter, and in the tropics or the North Atlantic.

Plimsoll line

The front of the ship is marked with a sighting mast. Otherwise it would be hidden from the crew in the bridge by the cargo on the deck.

Containers are stacked in racks on the deck.

GRACECHURCH CROWN

Save Our Souls

In an emergency at sea, passengers and crew put on life jackets and send an SOS signal. Rescue is carried out by a lifeboat crew.

Ship Shapes

The seaways of the world are busy with ships of all shapes and sizes.

Naval frigate

Roll-on/roll-off ferry

Oil tanker

Skimming Over the Water

Most water travel is not very fast because the water itself slows the boat down. But hovercraft and hydrofoils just skim across the water, so they can travel at great speed. A hovercraft is not really a boat because it hovers above the surface of the water. It is also amphibious, which means that it can travel on both land and water.

Water Rafting

People get around the reed beds and watery forests of the Everglades in Florida, in the USA, using flat-bottomed rafts. These have raised fan motors that do not get caught in the weeds.

What a Drag!

Water-skiers can speed over the water, but will slow right down if they fall in. This is because water is over 800 times denser than air.

The car deck will hold up to 60 cars.

This hovercraft can travel at a speed of 60 knots (111 kilometres an hour) in calm waters.

Propellers push the vehicle forwards.

Control cabin

The cars drive out of this door.

Up and Away

Hovercraft are also known as air-cushion vehicles because they float on a cushion of air.

When the hovercraft is sitting still on the tarmac the skirt is flat and empty.

The engines start and the skirt fills with air to become a thick cushion.

Hovering just above the surface of the water, the vehicle speeds on its way.

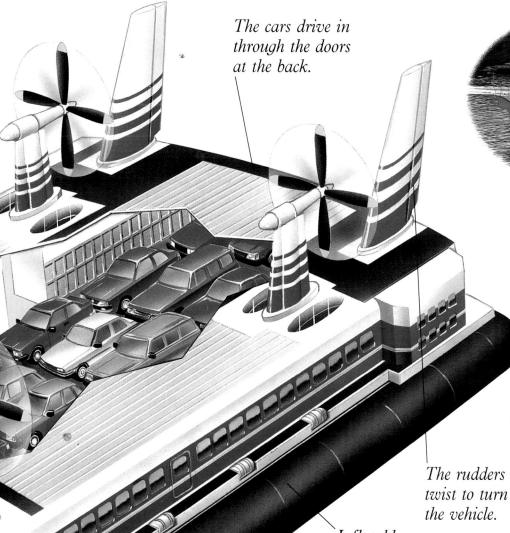

The cars drive in through the doors at the back.

The rudders twist to turn the vehicle.

Inflatable skirt

Air is sucked into inlets where fans push it into the skirt to lift the hovercraft.

A hovercraft like this can carry over 400 passengers.

Thin Fins

Fins under a hydrofoil lift it out of the water so that it can skim over the surface at great speed.

Riding High

Catamarans have two thin hulls so there is very little of the boat in the water to slow it down.

Super Speedy

Superboats have very powerful engines. They race at speeds of around 250 kilometres an hour – so fast that their hulls rise right out of the water.

UNDERWATER TRANSPORT

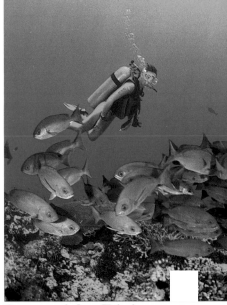

It is very difficult for people to travel under water, where the force of the water can be crushing and there is no air to breathe. But submarines have solved some of these transport problems. They are built from strong materials that are not crushed by the weight of the water. Modern 'subs' recycle water and air, and carry enough fuel to let them stay beneath the waves for two years.

Dressed for Diving
To keep them warm in cool water, divers wear wet suits. Divers also carry tanks on their backs containing air, which they breathe in through a mouthpiece.

Undersea Rescue

If a submarine has an accident and is trapped on the seabed, a Deep Submergence Rescue Vehicle (DSRV) is called to take the crew to safety.

1. A special transporter plane takes the DSRV to the nearest port. Here it is loaded onto a ship or a 'mother' submarine.

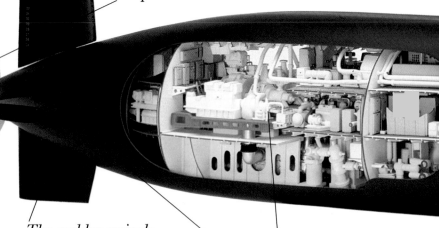

Propeller

The rudder swivels and steers the submarine to the left or right.

Engine room

2. The mother submarine takes the DSRV to the scene of the accident.

The hydroplanes tilt to make the submarine dive or rise.

The DSRV has to make several trips to rescue all the crew.

3. The DSRV locks on to a special hatch on top of the submarine, so the crew can climb into the rescue vehicle.

Scooting About

For extra speed, divers can use underwater scooters, which pull them along much faster than they could swim.

The periscope is only used when the submarine is near the surface.

Dangers of the Deep

For deep-sea work, extra protection is needed from the crushing pressure of the water. So small, reinforced submersibles and sometimes special, strong diving suits are used.

This is a nuclear submarine. It has a crew of around 140.

'Mess' or lounge for the junior crew

When the submarine is on the surface, the captain can command from the bridge of the conning tower.

This submarine is 83 metres long and travels at more than 25 knots (46 km/h).

Wardroom or lounge for senior officers

On Duty

As soon as the submarine begins to dive, the captain and crew in the control room rely on computers and electronic equipment to help them navigate.

Listening Out

Submarines find their way by using sonar. The submarine sends out a sound and then measures its echo. If the sound bounces back quickly, it means that there is an object nearby.

AIRSHIPS AND BALLOONS

Air travel began in balloons. Since medieval times, people have known that hot air rises because it is lighter than cold air. But it was not until the late 18th century that people developed hot-air balloons – huge bags of light material that float when filled with hot air. Airships were invented in the early 20th century. Unlike balloons, airships can be steered and were soon used to fly passengers across the Atlantic.

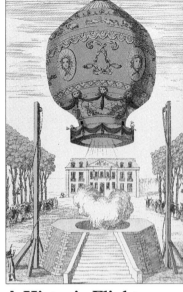

A Historic Flight
In 1783, the Montgolfier brothers made a hot-air balloon out of paper. It carried them 9 km across Paris and was the first time people had flown.

The Hindenburg *was three times longer than a jumbo jet!*

Sky Giant
The longest airship ever built was the German zeppelin *Hindenburg*. For twelve months it carried passengers across the Atlantic.

Air Disaster
In 1937 the *Hindenburg* burst into flames in New Jersey, USA, killing 36 people. This disaster marked the end of the great age of the airship.

Up in the Air
Getting a hot-air balloon off the ground is harder than it looks.

The crew use fans to fill up the envelope with cold air.

Airships Today
Many early airships were filled with hydrogen, which was flammable. Modern airships use helium, which is completely safe.

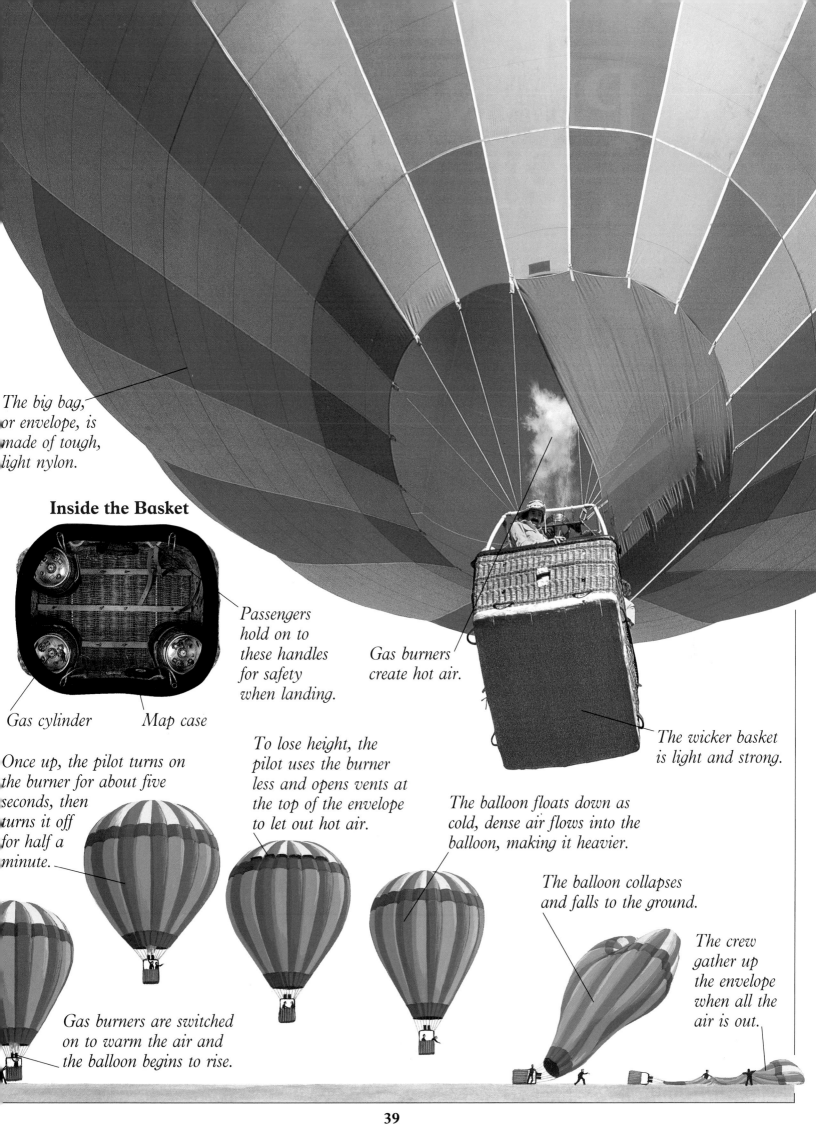

The big bag, or envelope, is made of tough, light nylon.

Inside the Basket

Gas cylinder

Map case

Passengers hold on to these handles for safety when landing.

Gas burners create hot air.

The wicker basket is light and strong.

Once up, the pilot turns on the burner for about five seconds, then turns it off for half a minute.

To lose height, the pilot uses the burner less and opens vents at the top of the envelope to let out hot air.

The balloon floats down as cold, dense air flows into the balloon, making it heavier.

The balloon collapses and falls to the ground.

Gas burners are switched on to warm the air and the balloon begins to rise.

The crew gather up the envelope when all the air is out.

PLANES WITH PROPELLERS

For hundreds of years people tried in all sorts of crazy ways to fly like birds and insects. But it was not until 1903, when the Wright brothers fixed a propeller to a small petrol engine, that people first managed to control a plane's take-off and landing. Today, huge jet planes can fly hundreds of people around the world, but smaller, cheaper planes with propellers are still the best form of transport for many jobs.

These propellers have three blades. As they spin round, they move the plane forwards.

Skis have been fixed to the wheels so the plane can land and take off from the snow.

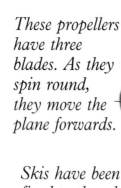

Open cockpit

Fresh Air!
In 1927 Charles Lindbergh made the first nonstop solo flight across the Atlantic in the *Spirit of St Louis*. Like all pilots at that time, Lindbergh had to wear warm leather flying gear such as a helmet, gloves, a coat and boots to protect himself from the cold.

To the Rescue
Light aircraft are relatively cheap to run and are ideal for transport in large remote areas. In parts of Africa, for example, the only way doctors can get to their patients quickly is by plane.

Short Take-Off

Small planes only need short runways. This means they can go to places where larger planes could not land, like this grassy airstrip on a mountainside in Nepal.

War and Peace

Over the years, there have been many types of propeller-driven aircraft.

World War I triplane

This plane can seat up to 19 passengers.

The rudder moves the plane to the left or the right.

World War II Spitfire

This tailplane keeps the plane stable. Hinged flaps at the back of it move up and down to make the plane climb or dive.

This twin-engined 'Otter' can take off and land in a small space.

Cessna light plane

Floatplane

Fighting Flames

This Canadair plane is specially designed for fighting forest fires.

The pilot prepares to lower two pipes to scoop up water into the body of the plane.

Flying slowly and quite low, the pilot opens a hatch to release the water.

As the plane skims the surface, up to 6,400 litres of water are forced into the tanks in 10 seconds.

PASSENGER PLANES

Join the Queue
The busiest airport in the world is Chicago O'Hare in America. Around 110 aircraft arrive or depart each hour. As at many busy airports, planes have to queue up at a 'holding point' before they can take off.

The biggest airliner today is the Boeing 747, which can carry around 500 passengers. Because of its size and powerful jet engines it is called the jumbo jet. Big planes have made flying much cheaper, and millions of people pass through the world's airports each year. The passengers simply step onto a waiting plane, but many jobs must be done to ensure every flight takes off and lands safely.

A Job for Batman
Once a plane has landed, a marshaller helps to park it by signalling instructions to the pilot with brightly coloured bats.

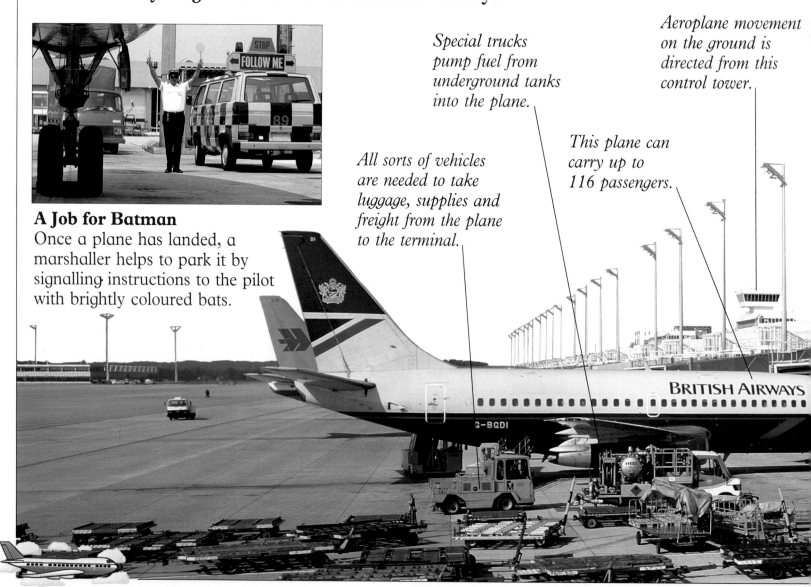

Special trucks pump fuel from underground tanks into the plane.

Aeroplane movement on the ground is directed from this control tower.

All sorts of vehicles are needed to take luggage, supplies and freight from the plane to the terminal.

This plane can carry up to 116 passengers.

BRITISH AIRWAYS

Supersonic

The fastest passenger plane today is Concorde, which has a cruising speed of 2,150 kilometres an hour. Because this is faster than the speed of sound, it is called a supersonic plane.

A Room with a View

At peak hours in major international airports planes are landing almost every 60 seconds, while other planes wait to take off. The take-off and landing of these planes is carefully supervised from the control tower.

Curious Cargo

Goods may be loaded onto a plane with a scissor-action crane or a conveyor belt. Some cargo simply walks in and out of the hold!

A Good Check Up

Before each journey the ground crew give the plane a good clean, inside and sometimes outside! Engineers check that the plane is in perfect working order.

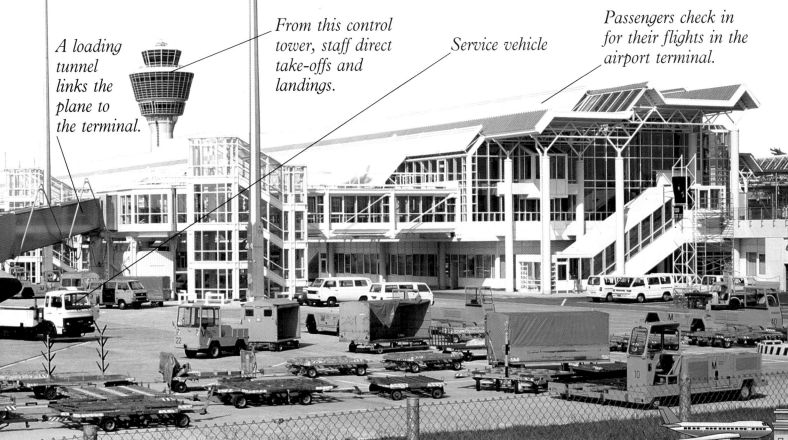

A loading tunnel links the plane to the terminal.

From this control tower, staff direct take-offs and landings.

Service vehicle

Passengers check in for their flights in the airport terminal.

UNUSUAL AIRCRAFT

Guppy transporter plane

Modern aircraft can perform extraordinary feats and are so complex that the pilots need computers to help control them. Some military planes are so incredibly fast that they can even catch up with the missiles they have just fired! Other planes are able to hover like helicopters, and then zoom off at great speed.

A Flying Fill-Up
On long flights, helicopters and planes may not be able to land and refuel. Instead, they can link up with a tanker plane in mid-air and fill up using special fuel lines.

2. As the plane rises the nozzles turn, pushing the plane forwards as well as up.

3. The nozzles then turn fully back and the plane uses all its power to move straight ahead.

Jumping Jets!
The Harrier is specially designed to take off vertically, like a helicopter. But once it is in the air, it flies like a normal plane and has a top speed of around 1,180 kilometres an hour.

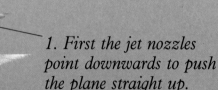

1. First the jet nozzles point downwards to push the plane straight up.

Short Take-Off
The runways on the decks of aircraft carriers are very short. Most planes are launched with a catapult, which shoots them down the runway to help give them enough speed to take off before the runway ends!

Optica low-speed observation plane

Sikorsky skycrane

The main rotor blades are turned by the engine to lift the aircraft.

Helicopters are noisy and shake a lot. But they can hover and so are ideal for rescue work.

The tail rotor stops the helicopter swinging round with the main rotor blades. It also steers the aircraft.

The body of the aircraft is called the fuselage.

ROYAL NAVY RESCUE

Rescue helicopters are fitted with medical equipment so that people can be given immediate treatment.

Helicopters need a lot of fuel and are expensive to run. This is because the main rotor, which keeps them in the air, uses a lot of engine power.

An airman is lowered by a winch to lift the victim to safety with a harness.

Swing Wings
Planes like the F14 Tomcat have wings that can change their shape as they fly. When flying at low speed, the wings are spread out wide, but they swing back for high-speed flying.

Low speed

High speed

MOVING INTO THE FUTURE

Transport never stands still – it changes all the time. Some changes are small, such as making cars, planes and trains safer, faster and more comfortable. Other ideas are more incredible. For example, in years to come, space planes may be a popular form of travel! Two things are certain, all types of transport in the future will try to use less fuel and produce less pollution.

Passengers have room to stretch out their legs.

Waste Not, Want Not
Each year about 35 million cars are made worldwide, using enormous amounts of energy and raw materials. In the near future up to 95 per cent of the metal, plastic, rubber and glass in every car will be melted down and used again.

Shape of Things to Come
This unusual car, called the BMW Z13, is still being tested but one day you may see similar cars on the road.

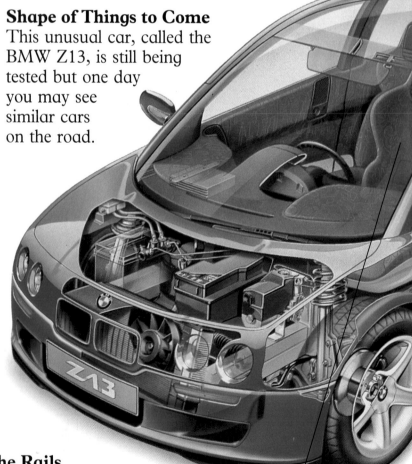

Off the Rails
Maglev (magnetic levitation) trains don't have any wheels. Instead, they are held above the track by magnets. One day, Maglevs similar to this German Transrapid will be designed to reach speeds of more than 600 kilometres an hour.

The front seat is in the centre so the driver has an excellent all-round view.

Two Hulls are Better than One

Ships use little energy for their size, but are quite slow. In the future, many passenger ships may be designed with two hulls. Because less of the ship is in the water, they can go faster than normal ships, especially in rough seas.

Travelling Light

A bicycle's frame and wheels are mainly metal but soon they may be shaped from carbon fibre. This synthetic material is lighter and stronger than metal.

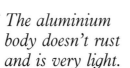

The aluminium body doesn't rust and is very light.

The Z13 weighs only 830 kilograms – about three-quarters the weight of an ordinary family car. So it uses less petrol and is faster.

Model for the Future

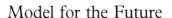

The Way Ahead

In-car computers are being developed that will help drivers to keep clear of traffic jams. A screen will show where the slow spots are and then tell the driver which is the quickest route to take.

Seeing Stars

Planes are now being designed that will take passengers into orbit. The American X-30, for example, will take off and land normally, but because it will go into space it should be able to fly to the other side of the world in less than two hours!

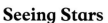

GLOSSARY

Accelerator A control used to make a motorbike, car or truck change speed.

Airbag An air-filled cushion that inflates to protect drivers when they are thrown forwards during car crashes.

Brake A control that slows down or stops a moving machine.

Bridge A raised area from which a ship is piloted and navigated by the captain.

Carbon fibre A light but very strong material that can be used to make bikes, boats, cars and planes.

Clutch A control that allows a car or truck to change gear. The gears help the engine and therefore the vehicle to work better.

Cockpit The front part of a plane where the pilot sits.

Container A big sealed box for transporting goods. It can be easily fitted to a truck or lifted onto a ship or plane.

Cutting A hole, shaped like a valley, that is cut through a hill to enable a railway or road to be built.

Diesel engine An engine that uses a type of oil called diesel, rather than petrol.

Engine A machine that produces power.

Escalator A staircase that moves.

Fireman A person who feeds the engine on a steam train with coal.

Freight The things, or goods, that are carried by trucks, trains or ships.

Gear lever A control for changing gear.

Harbour A sheltered place on the coast where a ship can anchor.

Hull The main 'shell' of a ship. Decks and cabins are put inside and above the hull.

Limousine A large and luxurious car.

Locomotive The railway engine that pulls the carriages or wagons of a train. Modern electric or diesel locomotives are called power cars.

Magnetic levitation Using magnetic forces to lift things. Magnets make Maglev trains hover above the track.

Pantograph A frame that picks up power from overhead wires to make trams and electric trains move.

Pedestrians People travelling on foot.

Periscope A tube with mirrors and glass inside it that is used on submarines for seeing above the surface of the water.

Pneumatic tyre A type of tyre that is filled with air. These tyres make travelling less bumpy.

Propeller Two or more curved blades that spin round to make ships and planes move.

Rudder A flat panel that is moved to the left and to the right to steer a ship or plane.

Semi-trailer The part of a truck that carries the cargo and is pulled by the front tractor section.

Streamlined Shaped to cut smoothly and quickly through air or water.

Tender The wagon of a steam train carrying the coal that will be burnt to release energy.

Terminal A building where passengers wait to get on, or go to after they have got off, a plane, train, bus or boat.

Tiller A handle or lever fixed to a rudder.

Tractor A vehicle that pulls things, such as trailers or agricultural machinery.

Viaduct A bridge that carries a road or railway over a valley.

Wheelhouse The part of a ship's bridge from where a ship is steered.

Wing mirror A small mirror on the outside of a car, truck or motorbike that helps a driver to see what is happening on the road behind.

Acknowledgments

Photography: Martin Cameron, Tina Chambers and James Stevenson at the National Maritime Museum, Greenwich; Andy Crawford, Mike Dunning, Philip Gatward, Dave King, Ray Mollers, Stephen Oliver, Dave Rudkin and Jerry Young.

Illustrations: Peter Bull, Roy Flooks, Alex Pang, Darren Pattenden, Josephine Martin, Sebastian Quigley, Eric Rome, Pete Serjeant, Clive Spong and Brian Watson.

Thanks to: BMW AG; Flora Awolaja; Emma and Thomas Gage; Donks Models; Islington Fire Station; Chris Lamport at Tamplins of Twickenham, London; Metropolis; Norrie Carr Model Agency; Renault; Scallywags Model Agency; Trafficmaster.

Picture credits

Air France: 43tl; **Allsport:** David Klutho jacket & 21bl, Gerard Planchenault/Vandystadt 7tr; **Archivio Veneziano:** Sarah Quill 28c; **Australia House:** 25bc; **Aviation Picture Library:** Austin J. Brown 42br, 43tc, 45clb; **BMW AG:** jacket & 46/7c, 47bl; **Bridgeman Art Library/Guildhall Library:** *Metropolitan Railway, Praed St., Paddington* by Kell Bros. 26c; **J. Allan Cash:** 18tr; **Colorsport:** SIPA Sport 35br; **ET Archive:** 30tr; **Mary Evans Picture Library:** 38cl, 38tr; **FBM Marine Ltd.:** 47tl; **Chris Fairclough:** 16bl; **Ford Motor Co. Ltd.:** jacket & 14tr; **French Railways Ltd.:** 25tr; **Colin Garratt:** 22tl, 23br; **General Logistics:** 47cr; **Robert Harding:** 8tl, 8/9c, 11tc, 17br, 18cl, 27cr, 45clb, 45c, MJ Bramwell 40/1c, Explorer 7tc, Robert Francis 18br, Nigel Gomm 19tc, James Green 41tl, Brian Hawkes 35tl, 35tc, 35tr, Chris Rennie 11tr, Sybil Sassoon 39t, GM Wilkins 35cra, A. Wolf 24bc & back jacket, Adam Woolfitt 28tr, Saul Young 44br; **Kit Houghton:** 8br; **Hulton-Deutsch Collection:** 8c, 8bl, 13tc, 13cr, 18tl, 22cl, 40bl; **Hutchinson Library:** 29c, Dave Brinicombe 9bc; **Image Bank:** Steve Allen 15crb, Grant V. Faint 24bla, Larry Gatz 16tl, David W. Hamilton 18bl, Chuck Mason 44cra, Tom King 34bl, Ocean Images 37tr, Co. Rentmeester 17cr, Holger Schoenbeck 24/25bc & back jacket, Milan Skaryd 42cl, Hans Wolf 19tl, 24bc; **Images:** 5cr, 17c, 28tl, 32tl, 33tr, 33cr, 42tl; **La Vie Du Rail:** 24cr; **Mansell Collection:** 12cl; **National Motor Museum:** 12tr, 15tl; **Panos:** Wang Gang Feng 10bl; **Planet Earth:** Gary Bell 36tr, Peter Scoones 37tl; **Popperfoto:** 40cl; **Quadrant:** 43cr, 46cl, Anthony R. Dalton 32/3c; **Renault:** 15cr; **Science Photo Library:** David A. Hardy 46tl, Peter Menzel 24tlb, NASA 47br; **Sea Containers:** 35crb; **Frank Spooner:** Rotolo Liais 25cl, Th. Barbier-Proken 40br; **Tony Stone Images:** Paul Chesley 26bl, Peter Correz 34c, John Edwards endpapers, Roy Giles 31cr, David Higgs 37bl, Barry Marsden 16br, Ian Murphy 32bc, Richard Passmore 16tr, Robin Smith 27tr; **Syndication International:** 6cl; **Telegraph Colour Library:** 1c & 16cl, 11c, 16/7c, 43cl; **Truck Magazine:** 21br, 21bc; **Zefa:** 7cl, 21br, 26tl, 28cl, 29cl, 31tr, 33tl, 34tl, 42/3b, 44bl, 46bl, Paul Barton jacket & 7cr, K. Benser 9bc, George Contorakes 6tl, W. Eastep 32bl, Richard Nicholas 43tr, Alexander Von Humboldt 30cr.

t – **top** c – **centre** b – **bottom** tl – **top left** cl – **centre left** bl – **bottom left** tr – **top right** cr – **centre right** br – **bottom right** tc – **top centre** bc – **bottom centre** tlb – **top left below** clb – **centre left below** cra – **centre right above** crb – **centre right below** bla – **bottom left above**